BEAUTIFUL CREATURES
Honoring Harambe
Celebrating Cecil
and Bringing Awareness of Endangered Species
by Spirit Wind
Artist Jude Bittner

IN LOVING MEMORY OF HARAMBE

I0423837

THIS BOOK CONTAINS 40 GRAYSCALE COLORING IMAGES

Grayscale coloring is a lesson in applying color, shading and contrast,
The shading in the images allow you to learn to apply color
to achieve real looking skin , fur and textures.

Featuring
Gorillas, Lions, Lemurs, Pandas, Owls, Bees,
Snow Monkeys, Orangutans, Rhinos, Iguanas,
Tigers, Wolves, Sand Cats, Butterflies, and Bees

BEAUTIFUL CREATURES

IN LOVING
MEMORY OF
HARAMBE

AUTHOR JUDE BITTNER OF SPIRIT WIND

ISBN-13: 978-1533647443
ISBN-10: 1533647445

Spirit Wind
Jude Bittner
Mason City, IA 50401
facebook: Spirit Wind, Spirit Wind's Creations Mason City, Ia
www.spiritwindcreations.com

THIS BOOK BELONGS TO

COLORED BY

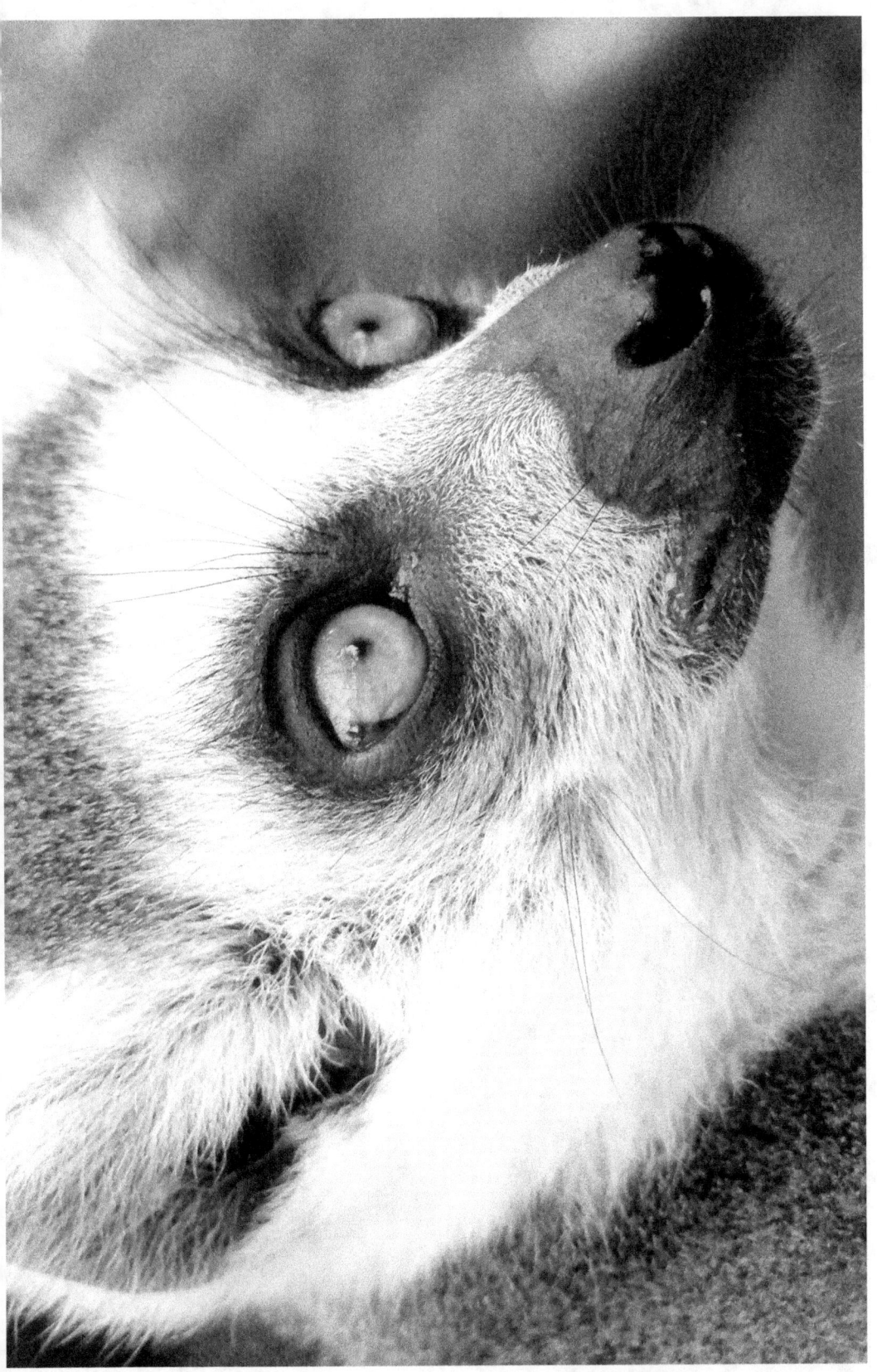

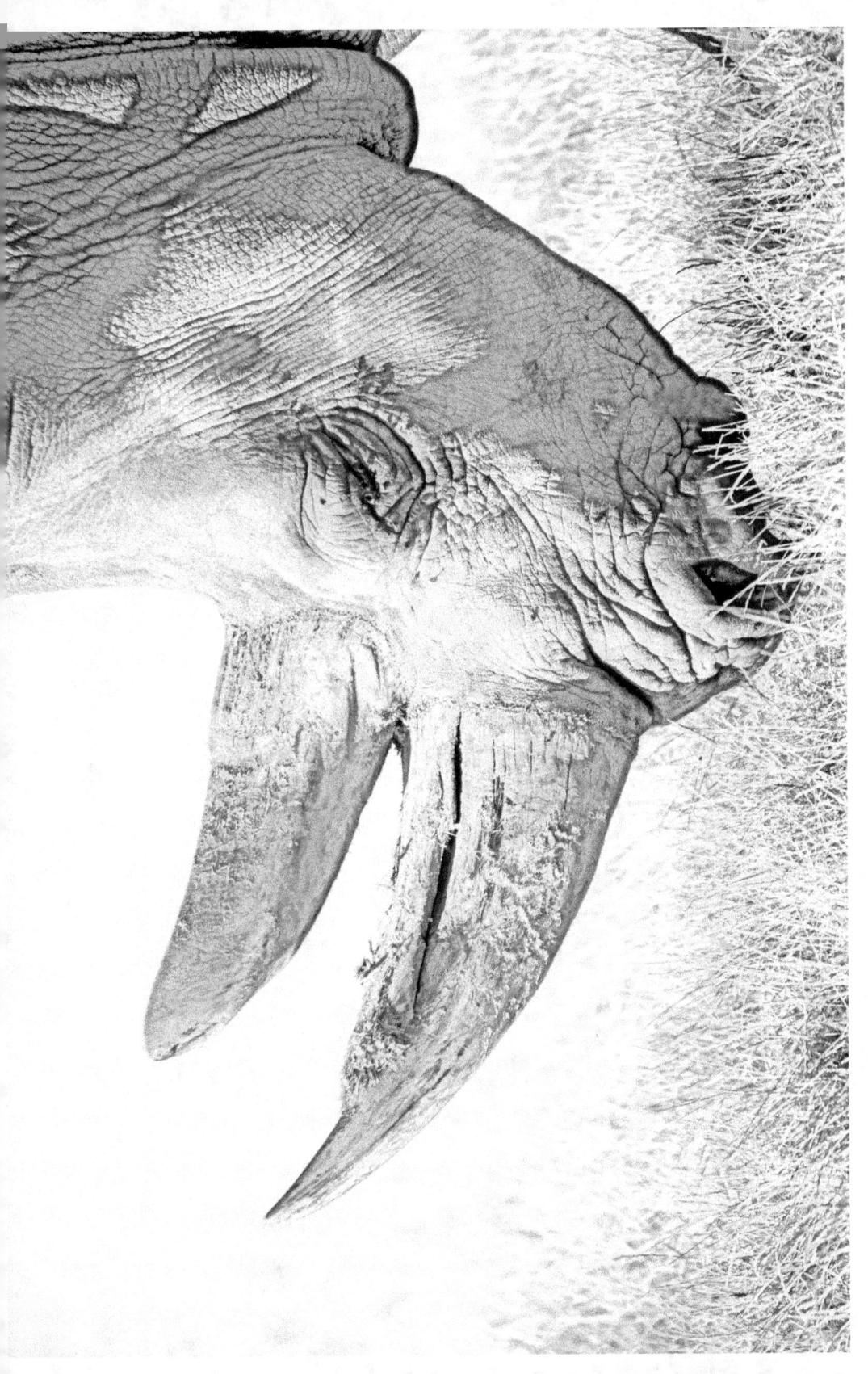

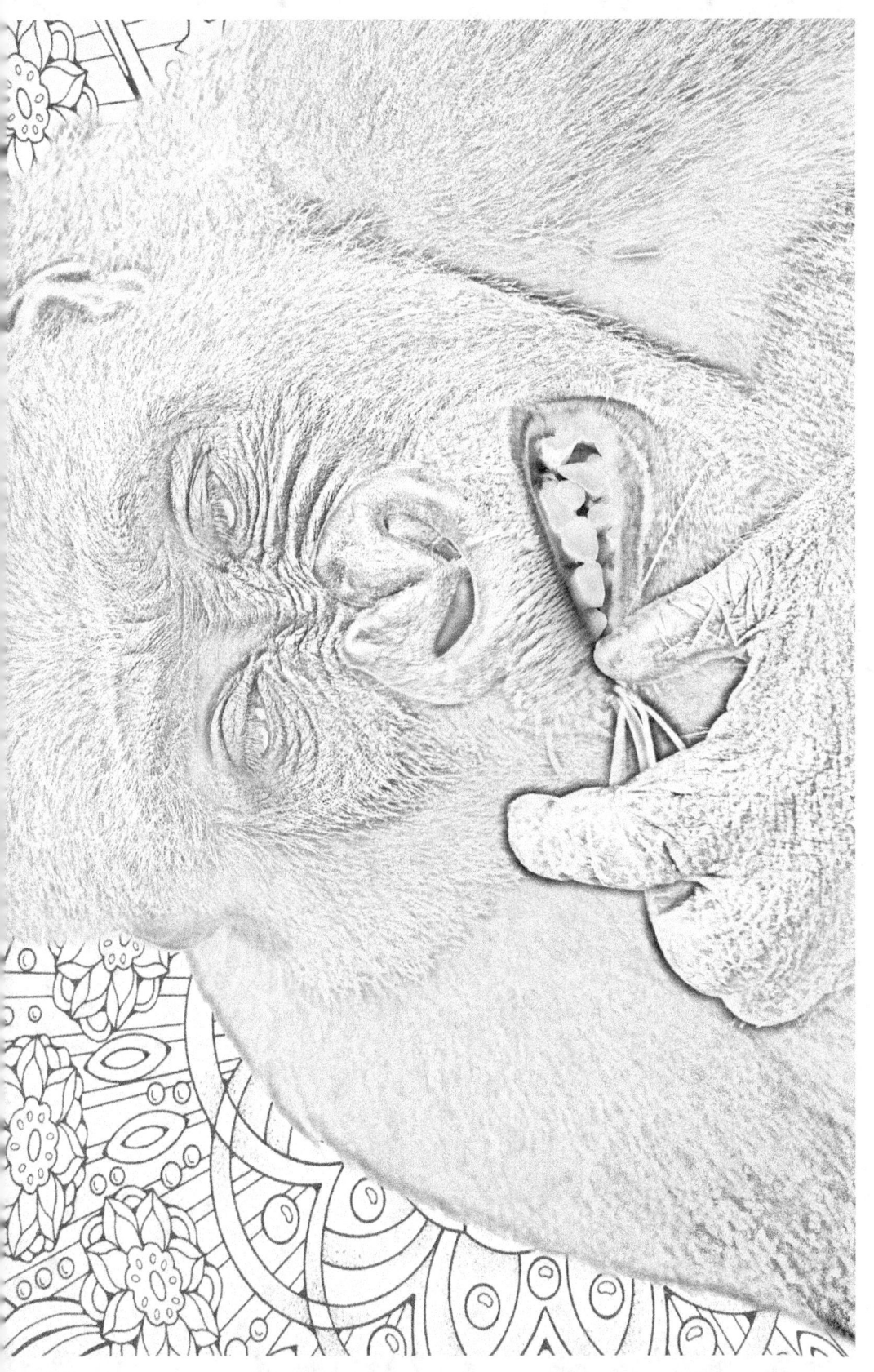

Be sure to check out our
tutorials for Coloring Grayscale Images

Have fun coloring this Fairy, she is in the "Adult Colorign Book Treasury... Collection 1

Please share your colored pages with me on facebook!
Spirit Wind's Creations, Mason City

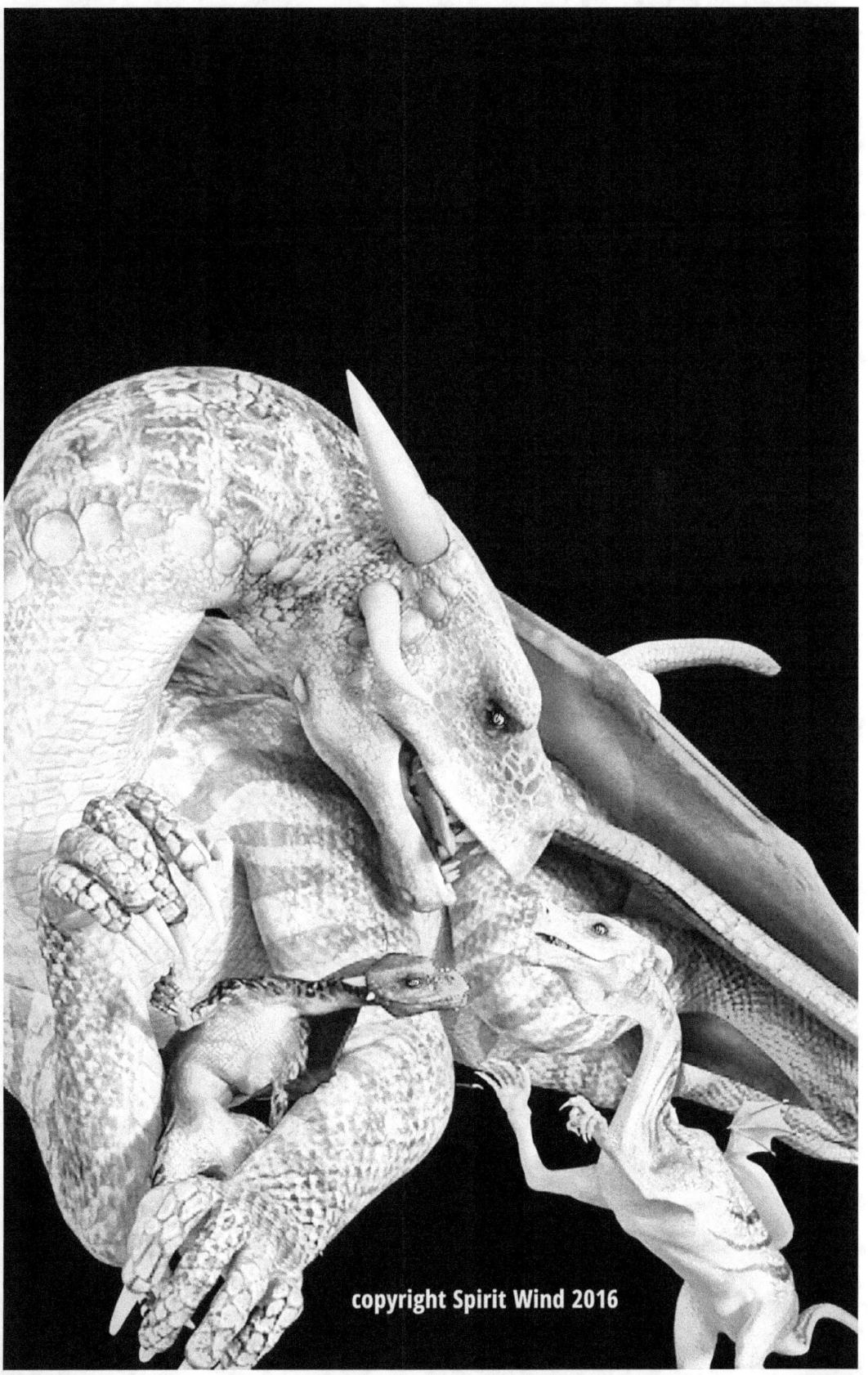

copyright Spirit Wind 2016

Grayscale coloring

Grayscale is the ultimate for learning to color. It is a lesson in color.
You can color using pencils, or markers.
We suggest you blend using the pencil itself with color. We have tutorials available at:
www.spiritwindcreations.com
and
Spirit Wind's Creations Mason City on facebook
Having the images
grayscale gives you a great base to color on and to blend with.

The paper used for these books is the best paper that you
can get through Createspace and Amazon.
We suggest you use a
blotter page behind your image as you color.
If you wish, you can reprint the page on 65 pound or 110 lb paper
for different results and mediums.
The images are copyrighted
so please dont share non colored pages on social media. You can however,
print on different paper for your personal use. We thank you
for acknowledging the artist's rights.!

We like to use colored pencils on the 65 pound paper and markers on the 110.

We look forward to seeing your colored images,
Please share them with us on facebook: Spirit Wind's Creations, Mason City

We have books and Coloring Pages availalbe
through our web site and facebook

Other Titles by
Spirit Wind

My journey in the arts began as a child.
I was the " Kid who was always creating something, Making a mess"
"Always taking the pictures"
From painting statuary as a child,
to being a Professional Sculptor and Potter.
The Call of the Arts was always there.
I love to sculpt and draw Fantasy Characters,
Having worked as a Professional Photographer for the past 12 years,
I have learned that life gives you Happy Accidents.
Learning about coloring books was one
of those Happy Accidents.

ENJOY, JUDE

www.spiritwindcreations.com
facebook: Spirit Wind's Creations, Mason City